Bandaged

Emma Filtness

ISBN: 978-1-915079-49-7

Cover designed by Aaron Kent

Edited & Typeset by Aaron Kent

Broken Sleep Books Ltd
Rhydwen
Talgarreg
Ceredigion
SA44 4HB

Broken Sleep Books Ltd
Fair View
St Georges Road
Cornwall
PL26 7YH

Contents

a winter sky of hot nude pearl
escape, escape
I have come here to heal

night roars quietly
I light a lamp and think –
of iron chains, memory, the city

its flora – beloved
I have snatched night
from darkness, from dust

*

in a flash my mind's eye shows me
a tormented existence
reflections, lies
a staggering mistake

the symbolic lovers
androgynous, inverted
the sweet anarchy of the body –
the body, sick

I have been deeply wounded

*

long sequences of light filtered
through the essence of dust –
sweet-smelling dust slaked with light
dust-red, dust-green, chalk-mauve

autumn inflaming the body
the flesh drunk-dark
shedding snatches of petals

hunt for nakedness
in those little cafes, the old poet
stirs under the petrol-lamps
disturbed by this desert wind

*

I had to come here to rebuild
the black ruins in metal
gold, phosphorous, magnesium
with slices of water-melon

in the open petal of the mouth
dusted by pollen kisses
lightly camphor-scented…

*

I am buried deep
in the shallow sand of madness
I believe in ecstasy, in suffering
I know, I know

*

in the quietness of the evening
the mind is licking its wounds
sulking along deserted beaches –
empty forever

grey cloud and shadow
wreckage washed up

*

alone, I have no name
I am cloudy, useless
wounded fragmentation
 – breath, skin, voice –

the house answers in a language
of its own invention

*

I live alone, sick
hopeless and haunted
pale, blue-veined, sullen

I dream vulgar dreams
spaces between time
a tide of dead things
powerful and deliberate

*

white-robed figures
like scattered paper, ringing silver
hot red glimpse of half-sleep

torn rags of flesh, some hidden
slaughter, the moans of a love-
song ground to powder

tired and blinking into pale hot light –
flowers of anguish, bandaged dreams
soft sad days

*

I glimpse the sea – a dusty silver flood
plunge softly, softly into the light

how touching, how feminine, terrific
queens, man-eating cats, acts of dirty love

*

a rare nightmare full of exotic charm
I approach the supernatural
a perpetual confetti of women

this animalism suits me
I have little books for company
I write to make love

survive with sadness
thoughtful and generous
night goes on long

I do not sleep well here
poor exhausted creature
wanting, touching, a woman feeling

I bear the burden of illness
haunted by a saturnine cluster
of intimacies

I glimpse the clumsy air, grappling
with ugliness
with deprivation

empty scent bottle
impregnated with memory
washed up, half-drowned

*

rotten, keeling
blood a black ribbon
flies in the eye of summer

the body violet, sweat-lathered
water-bearing sores like ponds –
my feelings overflow

I wait for omens
feel the cooling earth dip
towards darkness
possessed by desire

I remember the cheap perfume –
I don't know why

*

writer, lover, I recover
a sleeping woman in a cheap room
I awaken desire

a wound, a serpent
the healing unexpected, shabby
as the oceanic splendours of language

*

cult of pleasure
I enjoy intimacy
of a strange order

I discover simultaneous imagination
darkly woven colours of sensuality
a profound flirtation

I am cherub-haunted
this love affair a bitter scandal
in shark-skin, multi-dimensional

the poet speaks with tenderness
a love letter to herself, her body
(forgotten)

*

a black daffodil morning in this little world
carnal acts of metaphysical speculation

I am practicing the art of indulgence
tubular bells, brown bread
butter and almonds

gentle oracle, what madness
deep and lovely
translucent eyes
belladonna gaze

poet of gloomy verses distilled
shabby haberdasher, haunted
by wet lights and perfumed passions

a puffing damp, an ancient drizzle
the sea is awake –
I am overcome with a sudden longing
a lesbian irony

I heave a sigh of blue smoke
harsh light, wounds both
beautiful and horrible
fracturing silences

I forage for solace –
for love like a skin
a sort of paradox
summer fruit sweetness
bitterness

*

of goblin, of snake
virtue feigned, vice natural
as shark-coloured silk

a logical inheritance
an unlucky disturbance
an illness filled with hot winter pain

a half mad night
I sit half-drunk by the fire
finger the wound

*

I write by candlelight
pretentious-hysterical

*

Babylonian morning
wrapped like dead pharaoh
spread out like specimen

violet hair loose and vivid
sudden flights of poetry
a bottle of honey, lunatic wish

exhausted creature
distorted sorties
the light play of sex

watermelon gaze
the seeds inside stirring

*

dark metallic flavour of exhaustion
I am glass body lapped in silver river

poetry as clumsy metaphor
air glittering, the night sky sleeping

gravity is leaky, electric like Lucifer
tragic philosopher, manifest universe

I gather night deeply, deeply
the landscape responsive, comprehensive

tenderness and silence
a night so brilliant with stars

ghost-mauve sky, a dark, dark river
the body like thunder

*

A bat-flit night in the garden
the whisper of water, the lily-pond
      the sea
      the sea

night-hideous hubble-bubble
feeble light
ludicrous shadows
evil eye tears

clean bronze moonlight
crashing silver waves

*

ravenous autumn, uneasy phosphorous
long days of dust, lemon-mauve
star-radiant

rusty slag heaps
sand beaches glittering mauve-lemon
open sea the colour of oxidised mercury

melodious delicious
(breathless, breathless)
the evening sky savage
pressed like a bruise

I am doomed
my mind dream-like
body ripe, exhausted –
I know

carrion flower on the windowsill
a curious illusion
a delineation of the magical
the feverish

*

I move in the cobweb of night
shame everywhere
unearthed and ancient
harnessed to tenderness
trembling and tipsy
hopeless and burning

liquid, I write
into the blue
into the sea-gleaming
milk-white midnight –
morning star throbbing
above velvet waves

in the shabby simplicity of desire
I am lightheaded, foolish

in the gardens of intimacy
I ooze fragments of poetry

I know melancholy
lethargy for days

I lie with far-seeing eyes
like a sibyl

I am woman, poison-dark
rustle and babble

honey-sweating
dirty iron sweetness

creature dredged up
from the floor of unexplored ocean

*

this poetry is grimy
possessing ugly dispositions
frequent infestations

body out of order
I am blinded by smoke
briny and raving

I am maudlin hag
hysteric handbag
full of fragments

bulging with belladonna
rip-roaring like Cleopatra
unrolled

dark and swearing
ample and fetching
delirious and suffering

a haunted detachment
a shaggy shadow
full of flowers

a night-bouquet
of electric gold smoke
foul and delightful

conversations full of debris
the magical ease of the sea
a broken symbol

*

fruitless oracle
violet eye pouring curses

red-blue floating
piss-yellow wreaths of jasmine

heady herb-woman selling night
sulky, mysterious, bulging

with darkness, black copulations
axe through white flesh – poor creature

fragments of language
a body dreaming

      a death
      a death

*

(slippery kisses
haunted love)

*

I am influential
in some undiscovered fashion
figure large and florid

a silly little writer
this book is reptilian
half-dazed, savage

the text appalling
gilt-edged – guilt-edged
cheap narcissism

exhaustion brings coffee
a few flecks of hashish
a sexual curiosity

illusion of ocean
a leaking osmosis
a woman absorbent

citron-yellow, melon green
reptilian feelings buried
in the pre-conscious

fed dark jams and scented fat
I kiss the rigid penis
swollen with disaster

glittering and breathless
a savage caricature
pollen dropping hotly

bewitched woman
hunt for feeling
nymphomaniac indulgence

ego exaltations
smoulder explosions
I carry burdens...

bursting melodious density
hysteria like memory multiplied
unstop the bottle, take too many

I wish to untie
the psychopathology
of hysteria

a cuttle-fish waltz –
I dance badly, I confess
remorseless writer

a flirtation, moon-drenched
the sea in my mouth, desire
revulsion, exhausted imagination

such weariness, floating
suspended, a bedridden fortune-teller
hermetic, unhealed

an apology, a love letter

a sinking

silence

      silence

          silence

              a spell

*

I dream free from the burden
of form, the pattern organic
graceful and accurate

pale, rose-coloured, gold
I live in a nest of cobweb and old cloth
a writer isolated

I trace letters on a litter of paper
cutting in patched dressing gown
and velvet slippers snipping

portrait of the author as whore
the wound a shallow burden
infected by desire like original sin

call her nymphomaniac
she verges on Goddess
seeking temple

a rose, a shadow
decomposing cherub weeping
I write to remember

the light of the sun
a woman who only wished
to overcome this succubus psychology

I wish to be cured –
a creature breathing, alive
fantastic figment

a midsummer heat
rising damp of river
the stink of jasmine

a queer flushed light
bad dream, red light
I am an oracle-machine

physician-afflicted, treated
with nervous hesitation
I am puzzled examination

I tell a story
elucidate the mystery
miracles shaky as astrology

*

I read these pages
harsh-sweet echo
crude, rough-cast
sharp as black piano

I swelter in bed
visualise web woven
bray like stifled minotaur

soft linen, body naked
vanishing skyline of hurt

lustrous silence
compose the darkness

a little agony, sweetness –
cheap trappings

I am a little prayer
superstitious djinn

haunted invocation
soft, sensual spell

        of afternoon coffee
        and poetry

Acknowledgements

Bandaged Dreams is a poetry sequence created by applying the erasure or black-out technique to every paragraph in Part I of Lawrence Durrell's 1950s novel, *Justine*.

LAY OUT YOUR UNREST

Lightning Source UK Ltd.
Milton Keynes UK
UKHW010840101122
411908UK00004B/171

9 781915 079497